THE BEST 50
BRUSCHETTA RECIPES

Dona Z. Meilach

BRISTOL PUBLISHING ENTE
San Leandro, Californ

Printed in the United States of America.

ISBN: 1-55867-220-6
Cover design: Frank J. Paredes
Cover photography: John A. Benson
Food styling: Susan Massey

A STUDY OF BRUSCHETTA

The word bruschetta (pronounced either "broo-SKEH-tah" or "broo-SHEH-tah") is derived from the Latin verb *bruscare*, which means "to toast" or "to roast." Bruschetta is probably as old as Rome itself, but it has become part of the modern vernacular in Italian cuisine. Bruschetta traditionally was a slice of thick bread that was toasted on a grill or over a fire, rubbed with garlic, drizzled with high-quality olive oil and sprinkled with coarse salt. Making bruschetta gave Italian farmers the opportunity to demonstrate the quality of the season's new olive oils.

When people began to add chopped tomatoes, basil and olives to bruschetta, purists considered it heresy; they claimed that nothing should contend with the delicate flavor of the olive oil. However, these items, plentiful in the Italian countryside, soon became standard additions to bruschetta. Bruschetta was served as a mid-afternoon treat to satisfy hungry people who customarily ate late dinners.

Today, bruschetta can be served hot or cold as appetizers, snacks, main courses and with a little ingenuity, desserts. Usually, the topping is spooned onto a full slice of thick, hearty bread that has been toasted so that it is crisp on the outside and soft on the inside. Bruschetta can be served on a plate and eaten with a knife and fork, or the topping can be served in a bowl and scooped up with the garlic and oil-flavored bread.

Bruschetta can also be served as hors d'oeuvres or canapés. The toppings are placed on small rounds or squares of toast which are eaten with the fingers.

Seasonal tomatoes and olives were the choice of toppings in old-world Italy, but contemporary chefs also use mushrooms, fish, peppers, meat, chicken and more. A variety of sauces can flavor today's bruschetta, such as pesto, salsa, Alfredo and others. Flavorings such as basil, dill, oregano, thyme, salt and pepper are often used. Goat, Romano, feta, Parmesan and mozzarella cheese

can be added along with a touch of balsamic or other flavored vinegar. Creative chefs are taking bruschetta to new levels, assembling combinations culled from various ethnic cuisines. Dessert bruschetta has become popular, too.

A BUSHEL OF BREADS

In Italy, hearty country breads indigenous to an area are used for bruschetta. These breads are made only with flour, water, yeast and salt, and without seeds, sugar or fat. Generally, they have a non-porous texture that can withstand a drizzle of olive oil.

Artisinal Italian-, French-, Greek-, Vienna- or American-style breads that have a good crust are ideal choices for making bruschetta. Look for breads with names such as:

- *pane filone*
- *pugliese*
- *levain*
- *batarde*

- *baguette*
- *sflatino*

Sliced rolls, English muffins and focaccia also make fine bruschetta. Sweet breads, such as raisin and egg twist bread, are perfect for building dessert bruschetta. Avoid using thinly sliced soft white bread, as it does not provide the proper texture and density for bruschetta.

The type of bread you select will depend on its texture, size and how you plan to serve it. Usually, the bread is sliced about 1/2- to 3/4-inch thick, but a 1-inch slice can be used. Rolls and baguettes can be sliced horizontally for longer bruschetta. For canapés and hors d'oeuvres, the slices can be 3/8- to 1/2-inch thick so they can be easily eaten in one or two bites.

TOASTING BREAD

Ideally, the bread for bruschetta should be toasted on a grill, but toasting it in an oven, toaster oven or toaster will suffice. A small,

A STUDY IN BRUSCHETTA

round stove-top grill will also work. The toast should be crispy on the outside, its texture firm enough to withstand a rub-down from a cut clove of garlic, a drizzle of olive oil and a good helping of your choice of topping. One can also omit either the oil or garlic if a topping already has a good amount of these ingredients.

BASIC BRUSCHETTA

*True bruschetta is made from thick slices of densely textured
bread. Bruschetta can be served with simple accompaniments, both
savory and sweet. Figs, prosciutto or cheese are good choices.*

8 slices crusty white bread, ½- to ¾-inch thick
1 clove garlic, cut in half
3-4 tbs. extra virgin olive oil
freshly ground black pepper, optional

Toast bread and rub one side of each bread slice with cut side
of garlic clove and drizzle with olive oil. Season with salt and pepper to taste. Makes 8.

A STUDY IN BRUSCHETTA

STEWED TOMATO BRUSCHETTA

With a can of stewed Italian tomatoes on your pantry shelf, you can quickly create this delicious appetizer for an elegant dinner or for last-minute guests.

6 slices crusty white bread, ½- to ¾-inch thick
1 clove garlic, cut in half, or ¼ tsp. garlic salt
2 tbs. extra virgin olive oil
1 can (11½ oz.) Italian-style stewed tomatoes

Toast bread, rub one side of each bread slice with cut side of garlic clove and drizzle with olive oil. Top bread with stewed tomatoes. Serve at room temperature or heat in a microwave on HIGH for 1½ minutes. Makes 6.

FRESH TOMATO BRUSCHETTA

A simple bruschetta topping is, most often, the best. Savor fresh, slightly sweet tomatoes on this bruschetta.

3 medium-sized ripe red tomatoes, peeled,
seeded (see page 9) and diced
1/2 tsp. salt
1/4 tsp. freshly ground black pepper
1/4 cup chopped onion
1 tbs. chopped fresh basil
4 cloves garlic, cut in half
8 slices Vienna bread, 1/2- to 3/4-inch thick
1/3 cup extra virgin olive oil

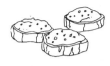

   In a small bowl, combine tomatoes with salt and freshly ground black pepper, onion and basil and mix well. Toast bread, rub one side of each bread slice with cut side of garlic clove and drizzle with olive oil. Top bread with tomato mixture. Serve immediately. Makes 8.

To peel and seed tomatoes: Drop tomatoes into boiling water for 15 to 60 seconds, depending on ripeness. Plunge tomatoes into ice water to cool completely. With a paring knife, remove peels. Cut tomatoes in half crosswise. Squeeze tomato halves over a bowl and use the tip of a spoon to remove seeds.

TUSCAN TOMATO-CHEESE BRUSCHETTA

In Italy, bruschetta toppings and the types of bread used differ, reflecting the foods of the region.

1 cup drained oil-packed sun-dried tomatoes, chopped
½ cup minced green onions
1 clove garlic, minced
½ cup pine nuts, toasted and coarsely chopped
3 oz. Asiago or Parmesan cheese, grated
8 oz. Provolone cheese, shredded
8-10 slices Italian bread, ½- to ¾-inch thick
¼ cup extra virgin olive oil

In a bowl, mix tomatoes, green onions, garlic, nuts and cheeses. Toast bread and drizzle with olive oil. Top bread with tomato mixture. Makes 8 to 10.

TOMATO-EGGPLANT BRUSCHETTA

Serve the eggplant topping in a bowl with a platter of toasted bread and let your guests spoon the topping over the toast.

1 large eggplant, about 1 lb.
1 cup finely chopped onion
2 tbs. extra virgin olive oil
1 tomato, finely chopped
salt and freshly ground black pepper to taste
12-15 slices French bread, 1/2- to 3/4-inch thick

Roast eggplant on a medium-hot grill, turning eggplant occasionally until limp, about 10 minutes. Cool and peel eggplant. Cut in half lengthwise, scrape flesh into a bowl and set aside. In a large skillet over medium heat, brown onion in olive oil. Add eggplant flesh and tomato and cook until mixture is heated through. Season with salt and pepper. Toast bread slices. Top bread with eggplant mixture. Makes 12 to 15.

TOMATO, BASIL AND CHEESE BRUSCHETTA

This is a perfect appetizer to serve on summer evenings.

1 lb. plum tomatoes, peeled, seeded (see page 9) and diced
2 tbs. extra virgin olive oil
2 cloves garlic, minced
½ tsp. salt
½ tsp. freshly ground black pepper, plus more to taste
3 tbs. finely chopped fresh basil
1 tbs. finely chopped fresh Italian parsley,
plus more for garnish if desired
¼ lb. fresh mozzarella cheese, cut into ½-inch cubes
4 slices French bread, ½- to ¾-inch thick
1 clove garlic, cut in half
2 tbs. extra virgin olive oil

Combine tomatoes, 2 tbs. olive oil, minced garlic, salt, pepper, basil, parsley and mozzarella in a small bowl and mix well. Toast bread, rub one side of each bread slice with cut side of garlic clove and top with tomato mixture. Drizzle remaining 2 tbs. oil on top and sprinkle with additional pepper or parsley, if desired. Makes 4.

SUN-DRIED TOMATO BRUSCHETTA

This combination has a hearty, tangy taste and appeal.

4 dry sun-dried tomatoes
1 cup boiling water
3 medium tomatoes, peeled, seeded
(see page 9) and diced
3 tbs. minced red onion
3 tsp. capers
3 cloves garlic, minced
2 tsp. balsamic or white wine vinegar
1 tbs. chopped fresh oregano

½ tsp. salt
1 tsp. freshly ground black pepper
24 slices Italian bread, ⅜- to ½-inch thick
¼ cup grated Parmesan cheese

Soak sun-dried tomatoes in boiling water until water cools. Drain tomatoes and chop finely. In a bowl, combine sun-dried tomatoes, fresh tomatoes, onion, capers, garlic, vinegar, oregano, salt and pepper and mix. Let stand at room temperature for about 1 hour.

Heat oven to 350°. Toast bread and top with tomato mixture. Bake bruschetta for about 5 minutes, or until tomato mixture is slightly bubbly. Sprinkle with Parmesan cheese and serve warm. Makes about 24.

TOMATO, FETA CHEESE AND MUSHROOM BRUSCHETTA

This bruschetta makes an ideal lunch or afternoon snack.

4 plum tomatoes, peeled, seeded
(see page 9) and coarsely diced
2 tsp. minced fresh basil
1 clove garlic, minced
salt and freshly ground black pepper to taste
8 slices Vienna bread, 1/2- to 3/4-inch thick
1 large clove garlic, cut in half
1/3 cup extra virgin olive oil
1/2 cup crumbled feta cheese
8 large white mushrooms, stems removed

Combine tomatoes, basil, garlic, salt and pepper in a medium bowl and mix well. Toast bread, rub one side of each bread slice with cut side of garlic clove and drizzle with $1/2$ of the olive oil. Top bread with tomato mixture, sprinkle with feta cheese and top each piece with 1 large mushroom cap. Brush remaining olive oil over mushrooms. Serve cold. Or, heat for about 5 minutes in a 350° oven and serve warm. Makes 8.

TOMATO AND PORTOBELLO MUSHROOM BRUSCHETTA

Portobello mushrooms are known for their rich, earthy flavor, meaty texture and giant size.

3 medium tomatoes, diced
1 yellow or red bell pepper, finely chopped
1 tsp. balsamic or red wine vinegar
salt and freshly ground black pepper to taste
1/4 cup extra virgin olive oil
4 portobello mushroom caps (about 1 1/2 lb.),
cut into 1/4-inch slices
3 cloves garlic, minced
8 slices Italian bread, 1/2- to 3/4-inch thick
1/4 cup crumbled feta cheese

In a bowl, mix tomatoes, bell pepper, vinegar, salt and pepper. Heat 2 tbs. of the olive oil in a large skillet over medium heat and sauté mushrooms and garlic until mushroom liquid evaporates, about 5 minutes. Remove skillet from heat and toss mushrooms with remaining 2 tbs. oil. Toast bread and top with tomato and mushroom mixture. Sprinkle with crumbled feta cheese. Makes 8.

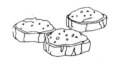

TOMATO AND WINE BRUSCHETTA

Serve these accompanied by a cool glass of white wine.

2 tomatoes, peeled, seeded
(see page 9) and diced
2 tbs. coarsely chopped sun-
dried tomatoes
1 tsp. minced garlic

½ cup dry white wine
3 tbs. extra virgin olive oil
6 tbs. unsalted butter
6 slices Italian bread, ½- to
¾-inch thick

Combine fresh tomatoes, sun-dried tomatoes, garlic, wine and olive oil in a small saucepan over medium heat. Cook, uncovered, for 5 minutes or until wine evaporates and mixture begins to thicken slightly. Remove from heat and stir in butter. Transfer to a blender container or food processor workbowl and pulse-blend on low speed until well mixed, but still slightly chunky. Toast bread and top with tomato mixture. Makes 6.

BRUSCHETTA WITH TOMATOES

GREEK-STYLE TOMATO BRUSCHETTA

These Greek salad ingredients make a festive appetizer.

3 large, firm tomatoes, diced
2 cloves garlic, minced
6 Greek black or green olives, sliced
1/2 red onion, minced
1/4 cup seeded and minced cucumber
1/3 cup extra virgin olive oil

1/4 cup balsamic vinegar
1/2 tsp. dried basil
salt and freshly ground black pepper to taste
3 French baguette rolls, cut in half lengthwise
3 tbs. crumbled feta cheese

In a bowl, toss tomatoes, garlic, olives, onion and cucumber. Mix oil, vinegar and basil in a small bowl and add to tomato mixture. Season with salt and pepper, mix well and chill for at least 1/2 hour. Toast bread and top with tomato mixture. Sprinkle with crumbled feta cheese. Makes 6.

TOMATO AND ARUGULA BRUSCHETTA

Use thin slices of bread for appetizer bruschetta. Thicker slices are key for a heavier luncheon dish.

4 ripe tomatoes, peeled, seeded and diced (see page 9),
juice reserved
1 bunch arugula, washed and cut into 1/4-inch pieces
1/4 cup minced onion
2 cloves garlic, minced
1 tbs. drained capers
1 1/2 tbs. balsamic or red wine vinegar
1 1/2 tbs. extra virgin olive oil
salt and freshly ground black pepper to taste
24-36 slices Italian bread, 3/8- to 1/2-inch thick
1 clove garlic, cut in half

In a medium bowl, combine tomatoes, arugula, onion, minced garlic, capers, vinegar, oil and just enough tomato juice to make the mixture moist, but not wet. Season with salt and pepper. Toast bread and rub one side of each bread slice with cut side of garlic clove. Top bread with tomato-arugula mixture. Makes 24 to 36.

TOMATO, OLIVE AND BASIL BRUSCHETTA

Garnish the serving platter with extra olives and basil leaves.

3 large tomatoes, diced
8 green or black olives, minced
½ red onion, diced
4 cloves garlic, minced
½ cup white wine vinegar
⅓ cup extra virgin olive oil

2 tsp. chopped fresh basil, or
  ½ tsp. dried
salt and freshly ground black
  pepper to taste
6 slices French bread, ½- to
  ¾-inch thick

In a bowl, combine tomatoes, olives, onion and minced garlic and mix well. In a separate bowl, combine vinegar, olive oil and basil and add to tomato mixture; mix well. Season with salt and pepper. Toast bread and top with tomato mixture. Makes 6.

TOMATO BRUSCHETTA, DIJON-STYLE

Use any flavored mustard to add a subtle twist to this bruschetta.

1/4 cup red wine vinegar
2 tbs. Dijon-style mustard
1/4 cup extra virgin olive oil
4 large tomatoes, peeled, seeded
   (see page 9) and chopped
1/2 cup sliced black olives

1/2 cup sliced green onions
18-24 slices French baguette,
   3/8- to 1/2-inch thick
1 clove garlic, cut in half
2 tbs. extra virgin olive oil

In a bowl, blend vinegar and mustard and slowly whisk in 1/4 cup oil. Add tomatoes, olives and green onions, tossing to coat well. Refrigerate mixture for 30 minutes to blend flavors.

Toast bread, rub one side of each bread slice with cut side of garlic clove and drizzle with olive oil. Top bread with tomato mixture. Makes 18 to 24.

TOMATO AND CHEESE PIZZA BRUSCHETTA

These mini pizzas work well when you need appetizers for a large crowd.

one 16-inch Italian-style flatbread, foccacia or pizza round
1 clove garlic, cut in half
1 medium tomato, chopped
1 clove garlic, minced
1 red or green bell pepper, coarsely chopped
5 tsp. minced fresh basil, or 2 tsp. dried basil
1½ cups shredded mozzarella cheese

Heat oven to 425°. Rub both sides of bread with cut side of garlic clove. In a bowl, combine tomato, minced garlic, bell pepper and basil; mix well. Spread tomato mixture over flatbread. Sprinkle with mozzarella. Bake for 15 minutes, or until cheese melts. Cut into wedges. Makes 12.

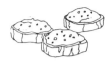

ARTICHOKE AND FETA CHEESE BRUSCHETTA

A fruity red wine is a fine complement to the sharp feta.

1 jar (8½ oz.) marinated
    artichoke hearts
⅓ cup crumbled feta cheese
¼ cup low-fat mayonnaise
¼ cup plain yogurt

8 slices Italian or French bread,
    ½- to ¾-inch thick
1 clove garlic, cut in half
¼ cup extra virgin olive oil
paprika

Heat oven to 350°. Drain and rinse artichoke hearts and cut into quarters. Mix artichoke hearts with feta, mayonnaise and yogurt and spoon into a small casserole. Bake for about 25 minutes or until mixture bubbles. Toast bread, rub one side of each bread slice with cut side of garlic clove and drizzle with olive oil. Top bread with hot artichoke mixture. Sprinkle with paprika. Makes 8.

PESTO AND MOZZARELLA BRUSCHETTA

When you can't find ripe tomatoes, opt to make pesto, instead.

2 cups coarsely chopped fresh basil, loosely packed
3 cloves garlic, coarsely chopped
½ cup pine nuts, toasted
½ tsp. salt
¼ tsp. freshly ground black pepper
¾ cup extra virgin olive oil
1 tbs. freshly grated Parmesan cheese
1 tbs. freshly grated pecorino Romano cheese
5 slices mozzarella cheese
8-10 slices Italian bread or French baguette,
½- to ¾-inch thick

Heat oven to 350°. Combine basil, garlic and pine nuts in a blender container or food processor workbowl and process on low for about 1 minute. Add salt and pepper about ½ of the olive oil until blended, about 30 seconds. Add Parmesan and Romano cheese and blend at medium speed until mixed, but still coarse in texture. Remove from blender and place in a small bowl. Beat in remaining oil, a little at a time, until the desired consistency for spooning.

Toast bread and top bread with pesto. Place ½ slice of mozzarella on each piece of bread and bake until cheese melts, about 2 to 3 minutes. Serve warm. Makes 8 to 10.

RICOTTA-MUSHROOM-ANCHOVY BRUSCHETTA

The anchovies add zest to the delicate bruschetta flavors.

1 cup thick tomato sauce
¾ cup ricotta cheese
¼ cup sliced fresh mushrooms, broken into small pieces
2 tbs. chopped red onion
1 tbs. chopped fresh basil, or 1 tsp. dried
8 slices Italian or French bread, ½- to ¾-inch thick
3 tbs. extra virgin olive oil
8 anchovy fillets, cut in half

In a glass bowl, mix tomato sauce, ricotta, mushrooms, onion and basil and warm for about 2 minutes in the microwave on MEDIUM-HIGH. Toast bread, drizzle with olive oil and top with sauce. Arrange anchovies crosswise over the top of each bruschetta. Makes 8.

GOAT CHEESE AND
BLACK OLIVE BRUSCHETTA

This recipe will taste best with high-quality brine-cured olives. They have more flavor than canned California ripe olives.

4 slices Italian bread, ½- to ¾-inch thick
1 clove garlic, cut in half
2 tbs. extra virgin olive oil
½ cup olive paste or pureed black olives
4 oz. soft fresh goat cheese, crumbled

Toast bread, rub one side of each bread slice with cut side of garlic clove and drizzle with olive oil. Spread bread with olive paste and top with crumbled cheese. Makes 4.

BRUSCHETTA WITH RED PESTO SAUCE

Red pesto, made with fresh tomatoes, is a favorite bruschetta topping in southern Italy.

2 lb. ripe plum tomatoes, peeled, seeded
(see page 9) and diced
2 cups chopped fresh basil leaves, loosely packed
3 cloves garlic, coarsely chopped
½ tsp. salt
3 dashes Tabasco Sauce
2 tbs. extra virgin olive oil
2 tbs. capers, drained and well rinsed
8-10 slices Italian or French bread, ½- to ¾-inch thick
1 tbs. freshly grated Parmesan cheese
1 tbs. freshly grated Asiago or Romano cheese, optional

In a blender container, combine tomatoes, basil, garlic, salt, Tabasco and olive oil and blend at low speed. Add capers and pulse-blend just enough to mix, but retain a chunky texture. Toast bread and top bread slices with tomato mixture. Sprinkle with grated cheese. Makes 8 to 10.

BRUSCHETTA PROVENÇAL WITH GOAT CHEESE

French bread slices covered with lightly browned goat cheese are a perfect prelude to a true French Provençal menu. Herbes de Provence is a traditional French blend of basil, rosemary, thyme, summer savory and lavender.

6 oz. soft fresh goat cheese
¼ cup whipping cream
2 tbs. herbes de Provençe
4 slices French baguette, ½- to ¾-inch thick
1 clove garlic, cut in half
2 tbs. extra virgin olive oil
2 tsp. chopped fresh parsley

Heat broiler. In a bowl, mix goat cheese, whipping cream and herbs de Provence, leaving mixture slightly lumpy. Toast bread, rub both sides of bread slices with cut side of garlic clove and drizzle with olive oil. Spread about 1 tbs. cheese mixture on one side of each bread slice. Broil 5 inches from heat source until lightly browned, 3 to 4 minutes, watching carefully so bread does not burn. Garnish with chopped parsley and serve slightly warm. Makes 4.

GOAT CHEESE AND ROASTED PEPPER BRUSCHETTA

Look for roasted peppers marinated in olive oil or vinegar.

4 slices Italian bread, 1/2- to 3/4-inch thick
1 clove garlic, cut in half
2 tbs. extra virgin olive oil
4 oz. soft fresh goat cheese, crumbled
1 jar (6 1/2 oz.) roasted red, yellow or
orange bell pepper strips

Toast bread, rub one side of each bread slice with cut side of garlic clove and drizzle with olive oil. Top bread with goat cheese and strips of roasted peppers. Makes 4.

STIR-FRY VEGETABLE BRUSCHETTA

This make-ahead stir-fry recipe will save you time during a busy work week.

1 tbs. extra virgin olive oil
1 onion, finely chopped
2 cloves garlic, minced
1 carrot, peeled and diced
½ cup finely chopped red
    and green bell pepper
¼ cup chopped celery

¼ cup balsamic or white wine
    vinegar
¼ cup chopped fresh basil
¼ cup crumbled feta cheese
4 slices Italian bread, ½- to
    ¾-inch thick
2 tbs. extra virgin olive oil

In a skillet, heat 1 tbs. olive oil over medium heat and sauté onion, garlic, carrot, peppers and celery for about 3 minutes. Remove from heat and add vinegar, basil, feta cheese and 2 tbs. olive oil; mix. Refrigerate for 4 hours. Toast bread and spoon over bread slices. Makes 4.

EGGPLANT-ONION BRUSCHETTA WITH FETA CHEESE

Eggplant and onions melt together and make a hearty winter bruschetta topping.

6 tbs. extra virgin olive oil
1 medium-sized red onion, diced
2 cloves garlic, minced
1 medium eggplant (about 1 lb.), diced,
or 3 Japanese eggplants, sliced crosswise
1/4 cup finely chopped fresh parsley or dill
salt and freshly ground black pepper to taste
8 slices Italian bread, 1/2- to 3/4-inch thick
2 cloves garlic, cut in half
1/2 cup coarsely crumbled feta cheese
balsamic or white wine vinegar to taste

In a skillet, heat oil over medium heat and add onion. Sauté onion for 4 minutes, stirring gently, until soft. Add garlic and cook another 2 minutes. Add eggplant and cook for 15 to 20 minutes, stirring frequently, until eggplant is golden brown and soft. Remove skillet from heat, mix in parsley and season with salt and pepper. Toast bread and rub one side of bread slices with cut side of garlic clove. Top bread slices with eggplant mixture. Sprinkle with feta cheese and balsamic vinegar. Makes 8.

GRILLED VEGETABLE BRUSCHETTA

Grill the vegetables on an outdoor grill or use the broiler in your oven.

½ cup prepared Italian salad dressing
1 clove garlic, minced
¼ cup chopped fresh basil, or 1½ tbs. dried
1 small eggplant (about ¾ pound), cut into ½-inch slices
1 zucchini, cut into ½-inch slices
1 yellow, red or green bell pepper, quartered and seeded
1 large tomato, cut into ½- to ¾-inch slices
8 slices Italian bread, ½- to ¾-inch thick
2 tsp. garlic salt
2 tsp. extra virgin olive oil
1 cup shredded mozzarella cheese

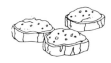

Prepare a medium-hot barbecue fire. In a bowl, combine Italian dressing, garlic and basil and brush over vegetables. Grill vegetables, turning once until softened: about 10 minutes for eggplant, 5 minutes for zucchini and bell pepper and 2 minutes for tomato. Grill one side of each bread slice until lightly toasted, about 1 minute.

Place bread toasted-side up (on a baking pan) and sprinkle with garlic salt. Drizzle bread with olive oil, top with grilled vegetables and sprinkle with mozzarella cheese. Transfer bruschetta from pan to grill with a wide spatula. Close grill cover and cook bruschetta until cheese melts and the bottom sides of bread are lightly browned, about 1 minute. Makes 8.

CURRIED OLIVE AND CHEESE BRUSCHETTA

Curry powder adds an exotic element to this flavorful mixture.

1 can (6 oz.) pitted ripe black olives, chopped
½ cup shredded mozzarella cheese
½ cup shredded cheddar cheese
2 green onions, chopped
1 clove garlic, minced
½ cup mayonnaise
1 tsp. curry powder
salt and freshly ground black pepper to taste
10 slices country bread, ½- to ¾-inch thick, or
5 English muffins, split
2 tbs. extra virgin olive oil, plus more for dipping, optional
1 medium-sized red bell pepper, cut into strips

Heat oven to 375°. In a medium bowl, mix olives, cheeses, onions, garlic, mayonnaise, curry, salt and pepper until blended. Toast bread and drizzle with olive oil. Top bread slices with olive and cheese mixture and place a strip of red pepper on top of each bread slice. Place bruschetta (on a baking pan) and bake for about 7 minutes, or until cheese browns, taking care not to burn bread. Serve extra olive oil in a dish for dipping, if desired. Makes 10.

ROASTED GARLIC SALSA BRUSCHETTA

Roasted garlic adds a smooth touch to this peppy salsa.

1 bulb garlic
2 cups diced tomatoes
1/2 cup diced green bell pepper
1/2 cup diced zucchini
1/2 cup shredded carrot
1/3 cup diced red onion
2 tbs. chopped fresh cilantro
2 tbs. lemon juice
1 tbs. extra virgin olive oil
1/2-1 tsp. hot pepper, such as Tabasco Sauce
20-24 slices French baguette, 3/8- to 1/2-inch thick

Heat oven to 350°. Remove papery outer skin from garlic bulb, leaving bulb intact. Place garlic in a small ovenproof custard dish, cover and bake for 35 to 40 minutes, or until soft enough for a knife to be easily inserted; cool. Peel garlic, remove pulp and chop. In a bowl, combine chopped garlic, tomatoes, pepper, zucchini, carrot, red onion, cilantro, lemon juice, olive oil and hot sauce. Cover and chill for at least 30 minutes to blend flavors.

Toast bread and top with salsa. Makes 20 to 24.

SPICY AVOCADO AND SALSA BRUSCHETTA

Fruit salsas are appealing toppings for a light bruschetta.

2 ripe avocados, mashed
1 tbs. lemon juice
salt and freshly ground black pepper to taste
2 tbs. purchased jalapeño or other flavor salsa
4 slices country bread, 1/2- to 3/4-inch thick
1 clove garlic, cut in half
1/4 cup extra virgin olive oil, plus more for drizzling
4 slices white onion, separated into rings

In a bowl, combine mashed avocados, lemon juice, salt, pepper and salsa and mix well. Toast bread, rub one side of each bread slice with cut side of garlic clove and drizzle with olive oil. Spread avocado mixture on bread slices and top with onion rings. Drizzle extra olive oil over onion. Makes 4.

ROASTED SHALLOT SALSA BRUSCHETTA

Roasted shallots have a sweet, unique flavor all of their own.

8 shallots
¼ cup extra virgin olive oil
1 tsp. minced garlic
½ red onion, finely diced
1 ripe tomato, finely diced
¼ cup chopped fresh cilantro
8 drops Tabasco Sauce,
plus more to taste
salt and freshly ground black pepper to taste
8 slices Italian bread, ½- to ¾-inch thick
2 tbs. extra virgin olive oil

Heat oven to 250°. Place shallots and ¼ cup olive oil in a small baking dish or ovenproof sauté pan and roast until soft, about 40 minutes. Cool and cut into quarters. Place shallots in a bowl with garlic, onion, tomato, cilantro, Tabasco, salt and pepper and mix well. Toast bread and drizzle with olive oil. Top bread slices with salsa. Makes 8.

SOUTHWESTERN BEAN BRUSCHETTA

Almost any type of beans can become a quick bruschetta topping with the addition of a favorite cheese.

1 can (15.5 oz.) black beans, rinsed and drained
1 medium tomato, chopped
½ cup chopped green bell pepper
1 tbs. finely chopped onion
1 tbs. chopped fresh cilantro
½ cup extra virgin olive oil
1 tbs. lime juice
½ tsp. salt
¼ tsp. ground cumin
½ tsp. dried oregano
1 tsp. minced garlic
4 English muffins, split
1 cup shredded Monterey Jack cheese

Heat broiler. In a bowl, combine beans, tomato, green pepper, onion and cilantro. In a small bowl, whisk together 2 tbs. of the olive oil, lime juice, salt, cumin and oregano. Add oil mixture to black bean mixture, toss and set aside.

In a small saucepan over medium heat, heat remaining 6 tbs. olive oil, add garlic and sauté until golden, about 2 minutes. Toast muffin halves lightly and brush evenly with garlic-oil mixture. Spread bean mixture evenly over 8 muffin halves. Sprinkle evenly with cheese. Place bruschetta in a broiler pan and broil 6 inches from heat until cheese melts, about 3 minutes. Serve immediately. Makes 8.

Recipe courtesy of Bay's English Muffins

AVOCADO-GREEN ONION BRUSCHETTA

Green onions and arugula add pepper to this creamy topping.

2 ripe avocados, coarsely mashed
1 tbs. lemon juice
salt and freshly ground black pepper to taste
4 slices country bread, ½- to ¾-inch thick
1 clove garlic, cut in half
2 green onions sliced
¼ cup extra virgin olive oil
1 cup arugula, coarse stems removed

In a bowl, combine avocados with lemon juice, salt and pepper. Toast bread, rub one side of each bread slice with cut side of garlic clove and drizzle with olive oil. Spread avocado mixture on bread slices and sprinkle with sliced onions. Drizzle a few drops of olive oil over onions and top with arugula. Makes 4.

CHICKEN BRUSCHETTA WITH PINEAPPLE-GINGER CHUTNEY

Chutney, an East Indian condiment, comes in a variety of flavors.

1 lb. boneless, skinless, chicken breasts, cut into 1-inch strips
½ cup finely chopped green onions
½ cup thinly sliced green bell pepper
⅔ cup pineapple-ginger chutney
3 tbs. extra virgin olive oil
6 slices country bread, ½- to ¾-inch thick
2 cloves garlic, cut in half

Combine chicken, green onions, bell pepper and chutney in a bowl and mix well. In a skillet, heat 1 tbs. of the olive oil over medium heat and stir-fry until tender, about 5 minutes. Toast bread, rub one side of bread slice with cut side of garlic clove and drizzle with remaining 2 tbs. olive oil. Top bread with chicken mixture. Makes 6.

STIR-FRY CHICKEN BRUSCHETTA

Make this appetizer and serve it as a full meal with extra bread on the side for sopping up the savory chicken juices.

2 tbs. extra virgin olive oil
1 lb. boneless, skinless whole chicken breasts,
cut into 1-inch pieces
6 fresh white button mushrooms, sliced
4 cloves garlic, minced
salt and freshly ground black pepper to taste
½ cup chopped red onion
½ cup chopped fresh basil, loosely packed, or 2 tbs. dried
4 medium plum tomatoes, chopped
4 tsp. balsamic vinegar
¼ cup grated Parmesan cheese
shredded fresh basil leaves for garnish, optional

6 slices Italian or French bread, ½- to ¾-inch thick
1 clove garlic, cut in half
2 tsp. extra virgin olive oil

In a large skillet or wok, heat 2 tbs. oil over medium heat and cook chicken until no longer pink, about 4 minutes on each side. Push to one side of pan. Add mushrooms, minced garlic, salt and pepper and cook until mushrooms are soft, about 3 minutes, stirring occasionally. Add onion, chopped basil, tomatoes and vinegar and cook for about 1 minute or until heated through. Stir in Parmesean.

Toast bread, rub one side of each bread slice with cut side of garlic clove and drizzle with 2 tsp. oil. Top with chicken mixture and serve warm. Garnish with basil leaves, if desired. Makes 6.

EGGPLANT AND TURKEY BRUSCHETTA

If you like, proscuitto or ham can be substituted for turkey.

3 tbs. extra virgin olive oil
1 medium-sized red onion,
    thinly sliced
2 cloves garlic, minced
1 lb. eggplant, cut into ¼-inch
    cubes
½ lb. fresh mozzaella cheese,
    cubed

3 tbs. red wine vinegar
8 fresh basil leaves, minced
salt and freshly ground black
    pepper to taste
8 slices Italian bread,
    ½- to ¾-inch thick
8 thin slices smoked turkey

In a skillet, heat olive oil over medium-high heat. Add onion and garlic and cook until soft, about 3 minutes. Add eggplant and cook for 15 to 20 minutes, stirring until eggplant is soft. Stir in mozzarella, vinegar, basil and pepper. Toast bread and top with eggplant mixture. Place a slice of turkey on each bread slice. Makes 8.

CHICKEN LIVER PATÉ BRUSCHETTA

Prepared chicken-liver paté makes an impressive appetizer bruschetta.

4 slices French baguette, 1/2- to 3/4-inch thick
1 clove garlic, cut in half
2 tsp. extra virgin olive oil
3/4 lb. chicken-liver paté, cut into 4 slices
1/3 cup low-fat mayonnaise
2 tbs. plain nonfat yogurt or nonfat sour cream
1 tbs. chopped fresh rosemary, optional

Toast bread, rub one side of each bread slice with cut side of garlic clove and drizzle with olive oil. Place a slice of chicken-liver paté on each piece of bread. In a small bowl, mix together mayonnaise and yogurt to the consistency of a thin sauce. Stir in rosemary, if using. Serve sauce over paté. Makes 4.

CHICKEN LIVER BRUSCHETTA

Serve these as appetizers for a small dinner party of four.

2 tbs. vegetable oil
1 small onion, thinly sliced
2 large cloves garlic, sliced
½ lb. chicken livers, trimmed
   and cut in half
1 tsp. freshly ground black pepper

1 tsp. salt
2 large fresh sage leaves,
   minced, or 1 tsp. dried
8 slices Italian bread, ½- to
   ¾-inch thick
3 tbs. extra virgin olive oil

In a skillet, heat oil and over medium heat and sauté onion until golden. Transfer onions to a paper towel to drain. Add garlic and chicken livers to skillet, cooking for 1½ to 2 minutes. Add pepper, salt and sage. Transfer mixture to food processor workbowl and process until coarsely pureed. Toast bread, drizzle with olive oil and top with chicken liver mixture. Top with sautéed onions and serve. Makes 8.

MEATBALL BRUSCHETTA WITH CHUTNEY

These appetizers can be made in record time by buying prepared meatballs and prepared chutney.

24 fully cooked cocktail-sized meatballs
1 jar (11 oz.) mango or mango-ginger chutney
½ cup water
8 slices country bread, ½- to ¾-inch thick
2 tbs. extra virgin olive oil

Place meatballs in a saucepan. Add chutney and water and bring to a boil. Reduce heat to low, cover pan and simmer meatballs for about 10 minutes over high heat. Toast bread and drizzle with olive oil. Top each bread slice with 3 meatballs and spoon chutney sauce over the top. Makes 8.

SWEET AND SOUR MEATBALL BRUSCHETTA

Two taste sensations merge and these meatballs come to life.

2 lb. lean ground beef
2 slices soft white bread, soaked in cold
water for 3 minutes and squeezed dry
1 egg, lightly beaten
1 tsp. salt
½ tsp. freshly ground black pepper
2 tbs. grated onion
1 jar (4 oz.) grape jelly
¾ cup ketchup
¼ cup water
1 tbs. brown sugar

¼ cup lemon juice
½ cup raisins
48 slices Italian bread, ½- to ¾-inch thick

In a large skillet, brown ground beef and pour off any excess fat. In a bowl, mix beef, bread, egg, salt, pepper and onion and shape into 1-inch balls. In a medium skillet, brown meatballs. Add jelly, ketchup, water, brown sugar and lemon juice. Simmer mixture over low heat for 2 hours. Add raisins during the last half hour.

Toast bread and top each bread slice with meatball mixture. Makes 48.

ALFREDO BRUSCHETTA

Assemble these ingredients for a cosmopolitan appetizer.

8 slices Italian bread, ½- to ¾-inch thick
1 clove garlic, cut in half
¼ cup extra virgin olive oil
½ cup prepared Alfredo sauce
1 cup thawed frozen cut-leaf spinach, squeezed dry
8 oz. prosciutto, thinly sliced
⅓ cup grated Romano cheese

Heat oven to 350°. Toast bread, rub one side of each bread slice with cut side of garlic clove and drizzle with olive oil. Spread bread generously with Alfredo sauce. Top with spinach, pressing down lightly. Top with prosciutto, place bruschetta on a baking sheet and warm in oven for 10 minutes. Sprinkle with Romano cheese. Makes 8.

SMOKED SALMON BRUSCHETTA

This variation on bagels, lox and cream cheese can be served as a morning delicacy or for brunch.

4 diagonal slices Italian bread, ½- to ¾-inch thick
1 clove garlic, cut in half
4 tsp. extra virgin olive oil
8 thin slices smoked salmon or lox
8 slices white or purple onion
¼ cup softened cream cheese

Toast bread, rub one side of each bread slice with cut side of garlic clove and drizzle with olive oil. Arrange smoked salmon and onion slices on bread and top with a dollop of cream cheese. Makes 4.

ANCHOVY, OLIVE AND GOAT CHEESE BRUSCHETTA

The olive spread in this recipe has the appearance and texture of caviar. The anchovy flavor lends a terrific bite to this bruschetta.

1 cup pitted black olives
1 clove garlic, roughly chopped
2 anchovy fillets
¾ cup pine nuts or walnuts, toasted
½ tsp. freshly ground black pepper
½ cup extra virgin olive oil
8-10 slices French baguette, ½- to ¾-inch thick
1 clove garlic, cut in half
4 oz. soft white goat cheese
1 red bell pepper, roasted, peeled, seeded and cut into strips

Combine olives and chopped garlic in a food processor work-bowl and pulse briefly to chop. Add anchovies, pine nuts, pepper and ½ cup oil. Process until mixture is slightly coarse.

Toast bread and rub one side of each bread slice with cut side of garlic clove. Spread a thin layer of goat cheese on bread and top with olive paste. Top bruschetta with red pepper strips and serve. Makes 8 to 10.

MIXED SEAFOOD BRUSCHETTA

Mild fish flavors and plum tomatoes make this bruschetta reminiscent of cioppino.

1 tbs. extra virgin olive oil
1 tbs. lemon or lime juice
1 tbs. snipped fresh chives
1 tbs. minced fresh basil
1 tsp. minced garlic
6 oz. frozen or canned crabmeat, rinsed, drained and flaked
8 oz. cooked medium shrimp, peeled, deveined
and coarsely chopped
1 cup chopped plum tomatoes
½ cup finely chopped onion
36 slices French baguette, ½- to ¾-inch thick
2 tsp. extra virgin olive oil

In a large bowl, stir together 1 tbs. olive oil, lemon juice, chives, basil and garlic. Add crabmeat, shrimp, plum tomatoes and onion and toss until coated. Toast bread and drizzle with olive oil. Top bread with seafood mixture. Serve immediately. Makes 36.

GRILLED SHRIMP AND
MANGO SALSA BRUSCHETTA

Pair mango with shrimp for a bright bruschetta topping.

2 French rolls, cut into 6 slices each, ½-inch-thick
¼ cup extra virgin olive oil
2 tsp. minced garlic
1 tbs. chopped fresh basil, thyme or rosemary
24 medium shrimp, cooked, peeled, deveined and tails removed
¾ cup mango salsa or chutney
chopped fresh basil for garnish

Toast bread. In a bowl, combine olive oil, garlic and herbs and drizzle over each bread slice. Grill shrimp for about 1 minute on each side, or until cooked through. Arrange bread on a platter and place 2 shrimp on each bread slice. Top bruschetta with salsa and garnish with chopped basil. Makes 12.

CAVIAR BRUSCHETTA

These will set the right tone for a memorable candlelight dinner. Assemble the ingredients just before you serve.

4 slices French baguette, $3/8$- to $1/2$-inch thick
1 clove garlic, cut in half
2 tsp. extra virgin olive oil
1 can (4 oz.) black caviar
1 tsp. chopped onion
1 tbs. chopped hard-cooked egg yolk
1 tsp. chopped fresh chives

Toast bread, rub one side of each bread slice with cut side of garlic clove and drizzle with olive oil. Top bread with caviar and sprinkle with onion, egg yolk and chives. Makes 4.

CHOPPED HERRING BRUSCHETTA

Buy prepared herring in sour cream for a fast, refreshing appetizer. This Scandinavian delicacy is one you will serve often.

6 slices Italian bread, ½- to ¾-inch thick
1 clove garlic, cut in half
2 tbs. extra virgin olive oil
½ purple onion, thinly sliced
1 cup prepared herring fillets in sour cream,
coarsely chopped
½ cup coarsely diced roasted red pepper

Toast bread, rub one side of each bread slice with cut side of garlic clove and drizzle with olive oil. Top bread with a thin slice of onion, chopped herring and diced red pepper. Makes 6.

GREEK BREAKFAST BRUSCHETTA

This bruschetta makes a nourishing morning meal.

6 slices day-old raisin or soft egg bread, 1/2- to 3/4-inch thick
3 tbs. butter, melted
2 tsp. sugar
1 tsp. cinnamon
2 cups chopped fresh plums, peaches or other seasonal fruit
1 cup corn flakes
1 cup plain yogurt
2 tbs. honey

Heat oven to 350°. Brush bread with butter and toast in oven until bread is golden brown. In a bowl, mix sugar and cinnamon and sprinkle over bread. Return to oven for about 3 minutes until warm. Arrange bread on plates and top with fruit, corn flakes and yogurt. Drizzle with honey. Makes 6.

MIXED FRESH FRUIT BRUSCHETTA

Your bruschetta will receive praise when served for breakfast or dessert. Substitute any fruit in season for those in the recipe.

8 slices day-old raisin bread, ½- to ¾-inch thick
2 tbs. butter or margarine, melted
1 tbs. sugar
2 tsp. cinnamon
1 fresh pear, peach or other fruit in season, diced
1 banana, diced
8 large strawberries, sliced, or ½ cup blueberries
½ cup plain or fruit-flavored yogurt
¼ cup honey
½ cup shredded coconut, toasted, optional, for garnish

Heat oven to 375°. Arrange bread slices in one layer in a shallow baking pan and toast in oven until golden, about 5 minutes. Heat broiler. Brush butter on one side of each bread slice. In a small bowl, stir together ½ tbs. of the sugar and cinnamon and sprinkle evenly over buttered side of bread. Broil bread about 5 inches from heat for 30 seconds, or until tops bubble. Remove bread from oven and place on a serving platter. In a bowl, mix together fruit and remaining ½ tbs. sugar. Top bread with fruit and yogurt and drizzle with honey. Garnish with coconut, if using. Makes 8.

BERRY GOOD BRUSCHETTA

Sweet bread and pie filling make a smashing dessert bruschetta.

8-10 slices day-old egg challah or other
sweet bread, 1/2- to 3/4-inch thick
2 tbs. unsalted butter, melted
1/2 cup nonfat sour cream
1 tsp. vanilla extract
1/4 cup sugar
1 can (16 oz.) blueberry pie filling
1/3 cup coconut, toasted

Heat broiler. Toast bread slices under broiler until lightly browned on both sides and drizzle one side with melted butter. In a small bowl, mix sour cream, vanilla and sugar. Top with sour cream mixture and blueberry pie filling. Sprinkle with toasted coconut. Makes 8 to 10.

BROILED FRUIT BRUSCHETTA

Fruit broiled on lightly toasted bread is a fashionable summer treat. You can also use seasonal berries for this bruschetta.

4 slices day-old country bread or sweet bread, 1/2- to 3/4-inch thick
4 tsp. butter, softened
1 tsp. sugar, plus more to taste
sliced peaches, pears, plums, apples or other seasonal fruit
3 tbs. lemon or lime juice
whipped cream

Heat broiler. Toast bread slices on one side under broiler until brown. Spread bread with softened butter and sprinkle with 1 tsp. of the sugar. In a bowl, combine fruit with extra sugar. Arrange fruit on bread slices and brush with lemon juice. Broil for about 4 minutes or until fruit softens. Cool. Top with a dollop of whipped cream. Makes 4.

STRAWBERRY-CINNAMON BRUSCHETTA

Use fresh or frozen strawberries for a rewarding dessert.

1 1/2 cups sliced strawberries
2 tbs. honey
2 tbs. chopped fresh mint leaves, or 1/4 tsp. mint extract
1/8 tsp. cinnamon
1 tbs. lime juice
2 tbs. butter, softened
4 slices day-old country bread, 1/2- to 3/4-inch thick
1 tsp. cinnamon
1 tsp. sugar
plain yogurt or sour cream

In a bowl, combine strawberries, honey, mint, 1/8 tsp. cinnamon and lime juice and toss gently. Chill. Toast bread until lightly browned. Spread bread with butter and sprinkle with 1 tsp. cinnamon and sugar. Top bread with strawberry mixture. Serve with a dollop of yogurt or sour cream. Makes 4.

INDEX